FOURTH ESTATE presents
BRYAN LEE O'MALLEY's

NOW
TURN THE
PAGE

5

26

PRECIOUS
LITTLE LIFE

JULIE'S NEW APARTMENT
A studio loft in what was once a warehouse or something. Julie shares the small apartment with three other girls because, although it is out of their price range, they knew it'd be the BEST place to throw the COOLEST parties.

Design by **Bryan Lee O'Malley** with **Keith Wood**

Published by **Fourth Estate**

Special thanks to:
Hope Larson
Intern Evan
TV's Matt Watts
Hugh Stewart
Shigeharu Kobayashi
Kanye West
...AND YOU

www.4thestate.co.uk | www.scottpilgrim.com | www.radiomaru.com

Originally published in 2009 in the United States by Oni Press
www.onipress.com

First published in Great Britain in 2010 by
Fourth Estate
An imprint of HarperCollins *Publishers*
1 London Bridge Street
London SE1 9GF

7

ISBN 978-0-00-793083-8

Printed and bound by CPI Group (UK)
Ltd, Croydon CR0 4YY

OKAY, UNDERWATER PIMP AND HO PARTY, CANADIAN POLITICS CIRCA 1972 BUT YOU'RE SECRETLY BATMAN PARTY, THEN THAT LAST ONE...

THAT ONE WAS HALLOWEEN, SO I THINK IT GETS A FREE PASS.

THEN WHAT'S THIS?

IT'S MY MEXICAN DAY OF THE DEAD PARTY, YOU RETARD.

DIA DE LOS MUERTOS!

MAN, JULIE, EVER SINCE YOU MOVED OVER HERE IT'S BEEN NON-STOP.

YEAH, WELL, NEXT TIME I'LL THINK TWICE ABOUT INVITING YOUR ASS.

WHATEVER...

HER OUTFIT IS *BARELY* EVEN THEME-APPROPRIATE. THIS PARTY SUCKS.

IMAGINE SHE DIDN'T INVITE YOU, THOUGH? WHAT WOULD YOU *DO?*

NO HORROR-THEMED MEXICAN FOOD, NO SLUTTY DEAD PEOPLE... YOU'D BE MISSING OUT ON A REAL CULTURAL BONANZA.

EHH, AT LEAST SHE'S TRYING. OR SOMETHING, I GUESS.

TRYING TO RUN US INTO THE GROUND.

...HELLO, BOYS.

MY GOODNESS. IT'S RAMONA FLOWERS.

HOW LOVELY. ARE YOU HERE ALONE?

SHE'S WITH ME.

AND THAT WOULD MAKE YOU... *SPOT PILGRIM.*

UH... IT'S SCOTT.

"SPOT" ISN'T EVEN A NAME, KEN.

UNLESS YOU'RE, LIKE, A DOG.

BALCONY
AIR QUALITY:
SOMEWHAT SMOKY

SO I GUESS YOU'VE DATED SOME REAL JERKS, EH?

YEAH, BUT WHO HASN'T?

TELL ME ABOUT IT.

YOU WANT A SMOKE?

NAH... I'M GOOD.

IS HE OKAY IN THERE?

C'MON. HE'S SCOTT PILGRIM.

SHFF

A TINY ROBOT IS KICKING THIS GUY'S ASS, IF ANYONE WANTS TO WATCH.

OH, AND THEN THE BAND'S GONNA PLAY.

WOW... LIVE MUSIC.

YEAH, MAN, AND THE BAND IS DRESSED UP LIKE *SKELETONS* AND STUFF.

CLEARLY NO EXPENSE HAS BEEN SPARED.

HEY, DIDN'T *YOU* GUYS USED TO BE A BAND?

WHAT, YOU DIDN'T HEAR? WE'RE RECORDING RIGHT NOW.

BLAM!

DEAD

TELL ME ABOUT IT.

I USED TO PLAY THE DRUMS, THREE TIMES A WEEK. MY LIFE HAD STRUCTURE. AND NOW... RECORDING. FOR *MONTHS.*

MAYBE YOU COULD TAKE UP KICKBOXING, OR SOMETHING.

CABER TOSS.

YEAH, OR I COULD JUST GO ON A MURDEROUS RAMPAGE!

VMM

VMM

TELL ME THAT'S AN EXCUSE TO GET OUT OF THIS HELL-HOLE.

EHH, NO... IT'S A TEXT FROM WALLACE WELLS. I'M LIKE THE PERSONAL SECRETARY FOR HIS LITTLE MASH NOTES TO SCOTT.

SAMSNUG

1 NEW TEXT

From: Wallace Wells

Hey buddddddy! Im a drunk 4 u. (U=scott)

Fri, 11:19 pm

REPLY Options

AWW. THAT'S ADORABLE.

YOU THINK SO?

UH, NO.

WHY AREN'T YOU GUYS PLAYING?

I TOLD YOU, WE BROKE UP.

SEX BOB-OMB *BROKE UP*?!

WHAT? NO. *ME AND JULIE* BROKE UP.

FOR LIKE THE FIFTIETH TIME.

SIGH

YOU CAN'T *STILL* BE PINING FOR HIM.

I — I'M NOT! IT'S JUST... WHEN HE'S WITH HER, HE SEEMS SO *HAPPY*.

WHEN WILL *I* BE HAPPY??

YOU KNOW HE CHEATED ON YOU, RIGHT?

WELL, YEAH, BUT...

HE WAS DATING YOU BECAUSE IT WAS *EASY*.

AS SOON AS RAMONA SHOWED UP, THAT WAS THAT.

I WAS EASY...?

HE TWO-TIMED YOU GUYS, AND HE ACTED LIKE IT WAS *NOTHING*. HE'S MY FRIEND, BUT COME *ON*.

ANYWAY, IT'S BEEN WHAT, SIX MONTHS SINCE YOU BROKE UP?

SEVEN MONTHS ON MONDAY.

YEAH, SEE? YOU HAD A RIGHT TO KNOW.

• • • • • • • • • •

WHAT ABOUT RAMONA? DOES *SHE* KNOW?

SWIG

AAAND...

I DON'T GET A PRIZE? NOT EVEN A *SNACK?* FIGHTING ROBOTS *SUCKS!*

THERE'S A TON OF FREE FOOD RIGHT OVER THERE.

GREAT. THERE GOES FIVE BUCKS.

THIS PARTY BLOWS.

HEY!

THUSLY.

CAN WE GO?

OH, HEY, IF YOU WERE PLAYING WITH MY PHONE ALL AFTERNOON, COULD YOU PLEASE CHARGE IT?

I WASN'T, BUT ALRIGHT!

WHATEVVERRR.

I THINK THE CHARGER'S IN MY DESK.

SHP

KIM'S ROOM
(ACROSS THE HALL)

OH MY GOD, I'M HALLUCINATING.

WE WERE HALLUCINATING WHEN WE STARTED A BAND IN THE FIRST PLACE.

SETTLE DOWN. WE HAVE A *SHOW*, OKAY? THERE, I SAID IT.

GUYS, I THINK I'M *HALLUCINATING*.

IT'S AT SNEAKY DEE'S AND IT'S ON SUNDAY. BIG DEAL.

THIS SUNDAY?

I HAD NOTHING TO DO WITH IT, ALRIGHT?

I THINK JULIE SET US UP IN A PETTY ACT OF REVENGE.

WHAT DID *YOU* *DO* TO THAT GIRL?

WE BROKE UP.

FOR LIKE THE FIFTIETH TIME!

35

TWO AND A HALF SUCKY-ASS MINUTES LATER

A SCHOOL DAY

I KNEW IT ALL ALONG.

CAN YOU ELABORATE?

LOOK. HE MAKES BAD DECISIONS... HE'S YOUNG! HE'S CONFUSED ABOUT LOVE! RIGHT?

SCOTT PILGRIM? HE'S *24*.

SHE SWOOPS IN, SPINS HIM AROUND, AND NEXT THING YOU KNOW HE STARTS ACTING LIKE A TOTAL A-HOLE.

SURE... YEAH... *THAT'S* WHEN HE STARTED.

I'M GOING TO THE GYM, PICKING UP DRY CLEANING, DEPOSITING MY PAYCHECK AT THE BANK, WORKING FROM 9 TO 3, AND I'LL PROBABLY GRAB SOME STUFF AT KENSINGTON.

YOU WORKING TODAY?

NOD

ALRIGHT, SO I WON'T SEE YOU UNTIL LATE. LOVE YOU! BYE!

· · ·

BOK

TEXT
TEXT
TEXT-A TEXT

Ramona
hates my
band!
What do
I do? >:O

TAP TAP TAP TAP TAP

VMM
VMM
flip

1 NEW TEXT

From: Wallace Wells

I hate your band
too, guy. Hey, we
should have dinner
sometime. And/or
breakfast. ;)

Fri, 10:03 am

REPLY Options

KLONG

YOU
BOOKED
OFF WORK
FOR THE
SHOW,
RIGHT?

DO WE
HAVE A
PLAN??

OF
COURSE
NOT!!!

OH MY
GOD, I'M
DREAMING.
WAKE UP,
WAKE UP,
WAKE UP...

OH, YOU'RE
ALWAYS LIKE
THIS.

ONCE
WE'RE ON
STAGE,
YOU'LL BE
FINE.

DOOMED

WE JUST *WERE*
ON STAGE FOR
SOUND CHECK
AND THE SOUND
GUY *HATED* US AND
WE SHOULDN'T
EVEN *BE*
HERE!

IT'S JUST
NERVES, MAN!
PRE-SHOW
JITTERS! PEOPLE
LOVE US.

WHAT... *SEX
BOB-OMB?*
I THOUGHT
YOU GUYS
BROKE UP.

46

WE'RE DOING "HERSELF" FIRST, RIGHT?

UH... YEP,

IS RAMONA COMING?

YEAH. FOR WHATEVER REASON.

I MEAN, IT'S NOT LIKE SHE LIKES OUR BAND.

DUMBASS, SHE LIKES *YOU*.

SHE'S SUPPORTING YOUR LOUSY ENDEAVOURS. DON'T KNOCK IT.

WHAP

...YOU'RE RIGHT. I GUESS I SHOULD BE GRATEFUL OR SOMETHING.

YOU'RE DAMN RIGHT I'M RIGHT.

KNIVES CHAU,
SUDDENLY

WE
HAVE TO
TALK.

...SO
TALK.

I'M STILL
MAKING UP
MY MIND
ABOUT
WHAT TO
SAY.

YOU MAKE *NO* SENSE, KNIVES. IT'S KIND OF AMAZING.

DON'T EVEN TALK TO ME.

NO, SERIOUSLY. I WISH I WAS EVER HALF AS FANATICALLY DEVOTED TO ANYTHING AS YOU ARE TO SCOTT PILGRIM.

RAMONA, HE...

HE CHEATED ON US.

BOTH OF US.

NO ONE ELSE WOULD HAVE TOLD YOU.

ZZLIP

YEAH, ACTUALLY, I GOTTA GO.

WHAT THE HELL IS GOING ON HERE?

OH MAN! YOU MISSED ALL THE ACTION!

DID I?

A ROBOT SCOTT PILGRIM'S ASS WHILE U WATCH

YEAH, APPARENTLY THIS WHOLE GIG WAS A SETUP! THIS ROBOT WAS SUPPOSED TO KICK MY ASS.

HOW DID YOU GUYS NOT NOTICE THESE FLYERS?

SO DO WE FINISH OUR SET NOW, OR WHAT?

SNEAKY DEE'S, NOVEMBER 14TH
ROBOTS PROVIDED BY
K&K KATAYA

GLANCE

THAT MAY ACTUALLY HAVE BEEN THE WORST SHOW EVER.

IT WASN'T YOUR FAULT, KIM.

IT WASN'T ANYONE'S FAULT!

YES IT WAS. IT WAS *YOUR* FAULT.

C'MON! AT LEAST WE HAD A GOOD TIME!

PLEASE DIE NOW, SCOTT.

HEY, DO YOU HAVE YOUR KEYS?

I TOTALLY FORGOT MINE AGAIN.

AGAIN?

DIDN'T I SAY I WOULDN'T LET YOU IN NEXT TIME THAT HAPPENED?

YEAH, BUT... YOU'RE RIGHT HERE. I MEAN, IT DOESN'T COUNT IF I'M *WITH* YOU.

DOES IT?

I DUNNO... GOTTA STICK TO MY GUNS, RIGHT?

ARE YOU *KICKING* ME OUT?!

WHAT? NO! C'MON. I JUST... I NEED SOME *ME* TIME, Y'KNOW?

IT'S A SMALL APARTMENT, DUDE.

NO, YEAH... GOOD IDEA. TAKE ALL THE TIME YOU NEED.

I'LL JUST SLEEP OVER WITH ONE OF MY MANY FRIENDS WHO DON'T HATE ME.

WELL, I'M SORRY THAT SHE KICKED YOU OUT.

WHAT? NO.

28

the GLOW

SHE JUST NEEDS SOME TIME ALONE OR WHATEVER.

IT'S A SMALL APARTMENT.

SO DID YOU DIG UP ANYTHING ON THE TWINS?

WELL, SEEING AS YOU COULDN'T EVEN REMEMBER THEIR NAMES, MR. HELPFUL...

WHAT? IT'S... RANDY AND ANDY... KATAMARI... OR... SOMETHING...

UH-HUH.

I DID WORK ONE MIRACLE, THOUGH.

YOU KNOW HOW MANY GUYS NAMED GIDEON THERE ARE IN NEW YORK CITY?

SHFF

PROBABLY A MILLION.

PROBABLY.

BUT THERE'S ONLY ONE FOR YOU, BABY.

WALLACE WELLS

WHAT? NEXT?

WHAT DO YOU MEAN?

SO ASSUMING YOU'RE ON TRACK TO BEAT THESE LAST COUPLE GUYS OVER THE WINTER, WHAT HAPPENS NEXT?

IN... THE... FUTURE?

LIKE, ARE YOU AND RAMMY GONNA GET MARRIED, OR...?

THE FUTURE? LIKE...

...WITH JETPACKS?

THE VIDEO STORE

LET'S GO.

WHAT'S UP? I WAS JUST GONNA COME INSIDE FOR A MINUTE, SAY HI TO HOLLIE...

YOU DON'T NEED TO SEE HOLLIE.

ARE YOU GUYS FIGHTING?

WE'RE NOT *FIGHTING.* I JUST—

...FORGET IT, OKAY?

LIVING WITH HER ISN'T WORKING OUT, EH?

WELL, WE DID EACH OTHER'S HAIR FOR A WEEK, THEN SHE GOT DEPRESSED AND STOPPED DOING DISHES AND NOW I HATE HER.

ADVERTISING! OH, YEAH!

STEPHEN STILLS' HOUSE
HOME OF STEPHEN STILLS and YOUNG NEIL

STEPHEN STILLS, ARE YOU STILL MAD AT ME?

WHY DON'T WE HANG OUT HERE ANY-MORE?

YOUNG NEIL'S ROOM

HE'S OUT.

WELL, WHERE IS HE?

I DUNNO, BAND PRACTICE?

WE'RE THE BAND, THOUGH.

WE'RE RIGHT HERE.

DO YOU SEE WHAT I'M SAYING?

• • • • •

THAI

KIM'S PLACE

THAT NIGHT

IS THIS GOING TO BECOME A REGULAR OCCURRENCE?

OH, NO WAY. THIS IS NOTHING.

OKAY. I MEAN, COOL.

WELL... 'NIGHT.

ACTUALLY... CAN YOU DO ME A FAVOUR?

69

the NEXT DAY

70

KIM?

KIM *PINE*?

FANCY MEETING YOU HERE!

OH... HEY, RAMONA.

SMOOTH

STARE

DID HE PUT YOU UP TO THIS?

YES.

LAUGHING HER ASS OFF

GOD, I CAN'T BELIEVE THAT *WORKED*.

ANYWAY.

WHATEVER HAPPENED TO THAT GUY YOU WERE SEEING?

YOU MEAN JASON KIM?

YOU WERE *DATING* THAT GUY?

I WAS.

DIDN'T WORK OUT?

WELL, HE KIND OF HAD A...

...*TRYST* WITH MY ROOMMATE.

73

DID I MENTION WE HAD A SLEEPOVER? ME AND KIM!

REALLY.

HE JUST SLEPT ON THE COUCH.

THAT'S COOL.

AND THE NIGHT BEFORE, I SLEPT OVER AT WALLACE'S!

BED OR COUCH?

I DON'T HAVE TO ANSWER THAT—

OKAY, AT THE RISK OF SOUNDING INSENSITIVE, RAMONA, *WHAT'S WITH YOUR HEAD?!?*

BUMP

JULIE'S APARTMENT: another friggin' party

EXCUSE ME.

YOU WISH, YOUNG NEIL.

WHO'S THE BROAD? I THOUGHT YOU WERE DATING KNIVES CHAU.

CHAU? THAT WAS LIKE YEARS AGO, RAMONA. ANYWAY, SHE'S OBSESSED WITH CAPTAIN HOMO THESE DAYS...

CAPTAIN HOMO. NICE.

HE'S AN ASSHOLE.

SO ARE YOU.

I'M YOUNG. I'LL GROW OUT OF IT.

PUT THE BOTTLE BACK, THIEF! THAT'S FOR LEGITIMATE PARTYGOERS!

CUERVO ESPECIAL?

SOUNDS LIKE OUR FRIEND RAMONA PICKED THE POISON.

AHH... GOOD TIMES.

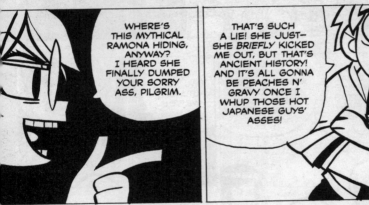

WHERE'S THIS MYTHICAL RAMONA HIDING, ANYWAY? I HEARD SHE FINALLY DUMPED YOUR SORRY ASS, PILGRIM.

THAT'S SUCH A LIE! SHE JUST— SHE *BRIEFLY* KICKED ME OUT, BUT THAT'S ANCIENT HISTORY! AND IT'S ALL GONNA BE PEACHES N' GRAVY ONCE I WHUP THOSE HOT JAPANESE GUYS' ASSES!

YOU'RE SICK, SCOTT. SEEK HELP.

I DON'T NEED *HELP*. I'LL TAKE CARE OF BUSINESS *RIGHT NOW!*

KTHUN

GRAB

THERE'S NO SHAME IN BEING YOURSELF, RAMONA. ALL THIS, HERE—

THIS IS TEMPORARY.

REAL LIFE'S WAITING.

SHFFF

the UNIVERSE
FIGHTS BACK

29

WHAT DOES IT MEAN?

photo_013.jpg

BACK

OPTIONS

KTONGG

NO IDEA.

RAMONA, COME ON. IF YOU CAN'T TELL ME, YOU CAN'T TELL ME.

SNAP

I WON'T BE OFFENDED.

OKAY...

I CAN'T TELL YOU.

SWIG

GRAB

WHAT THE HELL.

IS HE OKAY DOWN THERE?

C'MON. HE'S SCOTT PILGRIM.

WHAT'S UP, STUD? RAMONA'S GETTING WORRIED.

WHOA!

HOW'D YOU GET UP THERE?

TRY THE STAIRS.

TWENTY MINUTES DRUNKER

HEY, RAMONA...

HAVE YOU EVER DATED ANYONE WHO *WASN'T* EVIL?

Jose Cuervo Especial

NOT THAT FIGHTING HARDER AND HARDER BATTLES FOR YOUR LOVE IS GETTING OLD, OR ANYTHING...

YEAH, ONCE. THIS GUY DOUG.

HE WAS KIND OF A DICK, THOUGH.

EVEN YOUR *NON-EVIL* EX-BOYFRIEND WAS A DICK?

WELL, HE DUMPED ME.

UNCEREMONIOUSLY.

I'VE BEEN THINKING I SHOULD GO BACK TO SCHOOL.

OH, YOU TOTALLY SHOULD! I MEAN, SO SHOULD I...

WE SHOULD GO *TOGETHER*. WHAT WILL WE MAJOR IN?

DATING.

RUGBY?

ZOOLOGICAL ANTHROPOLOGY!

SHOPPING!

T—

TEQUILA!!

A WHILE MORE DRUNKER

YOU GUYS, SERIOUSLY...

...I SERIOUSLY LOVE YOU...

WHAT TIME IS IT?

IS IT HOME TIME?

SHUT UP, SCOTT.

I SERIOUSLY WISH I COULD... LIKE... *BE* YOU, RAMONA.

I MEAN, YOU'RE SO... Y'KNOW?

Smek

KIM PINE, WHERE HAVE YOU BEEN ALL MY LIFE?

MAKE OUT!

T. PATRICK

YOU'VE BEEN HERE ALL ALONG...

...HAVEN'T YOU?

99

HERE AT THE SUBWAY STATION?

CLEVER GIRL.

YOU STAND BESIDE HIM.

NO MATTER WHAT.

HE'S *IMPORTANT* TO YOU.

OKAY, YOU KNOW WHAT? GO FINISH EACH OTHER'S SENTENCES SOMEWHERE ELSE.

YOU GOT NO BUSINESS WITH ME.

DID YOU CHEAT ON ME?

IS THERE A DIFFERENCE?!

...YOU WEREN'T WRONGED?

FWIP

I GUESS I JUST THOUGHT YOU WERE BETTER THAN THAT.

YOU'RE A BAD PERSON.

SO DID I! I JUST... IT *HAPPENED.* I'VE BEEN TRYING TO FORGET ABOUT IT.

I'M—

——I'M A BAD PERSON!

YOU THINK I'M A BAD PERSON?

WELL, YOU'RE A LIAR AND A CHEAT...

I'M TRYING TO BE BETTER, RAMONA. I'M TRYING TO *CHANGE.* FOR *YOU.*

GREAT. GOOD JOB. YOU TRICKED ME INTO THINKING YOU WERE A DECENT GUY.

BUT YOU'RE JUST ANOTHER EVIL EX-BOYFRIEND WAITING TO HAPPEN, AREN'T YOU?

NO RAMONA

NO HEARTBEAT

SAMSNUG

1 NEW TEXT

From: Kim

Twins got me. In cage. Asst req. Const site Q+bath

Sun, 4:36 am

REPLY Options

UH-OH.

I HAVE TO GO RESCUE KIM, BUT I'LL BE BACK!!

DON'T BREAK UP WITH ME WHILE I'M OUT, OKAY?!

CLOMP CLOMP CLOM CLO

**CONSTRUCTION SITE
QUEEN & BATHURST**
An old building is being gutted
and turned into something else.

the GLOW,
part 2

30

WHAT'S
WRONG WITH
YOU?

TWIN-LINK

DOUBLE HURRICANE KICK!

KEN: $79.95
KYLE: $74.95
TWIN BONUS: $2.00

ACHIEVEMENT UNLOCKED!
DEFEATED THE TWINS SIMULTANEOUSLY

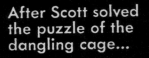
After Scott solved
the puzzle of the
dangling cage...

WHATEVER.
IT'S COOL.

I'M SORRY YOU HAD TO GET INVOLVED.

ARE YOU OKAY?

I AM SO READY TO HOP IN THE SHOWER.

WHAT ABOUT YOU? ARE YOU GONNA BE OKAY?

ONE MORE ASSHOLE TO GO, RIGHT? I SHOULD REALLY RUN HOME, THOUGH.

ME AND RAMONA, WE'RE—

RAMONA--!

WHOA, YOUR...

YOUR HAIR...

137

PLOP

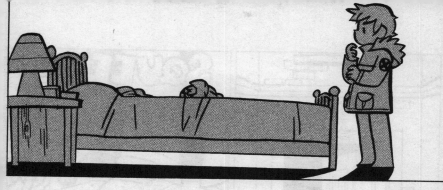

GIDEON.

RAMONA...?

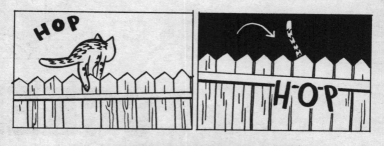

GAME OVER

CHOP CHOP CHOP

SCRAPE SCRAPE

AWW, SCOTTIE, THAT'S RIGHT, LET IT ALL OUT.

WHUH?

HEY! IT'S THE *ONIONS!* I'M NOT EVEN SAD, I'M JUST CONFUSED!

YOU MIND STAYING ELSEWHERE TONIGHT?

YOUR CONSTANT *NIGHT-YOWLING* IS INTERFERING WITH MY SLEEP.

YEAH, OKAY.

WANNA GRAB A DRINK, TALK ABOUT THE BAND?

NO THANKS. GOTTA DO A THING.

HEEERE KITTY...

HOW YOU DOING?

I'M OKAY.

UH, THIS IS KINDA EMBARRASSING, BUT, UM, HOLLIE SOLD OUR COUCH.

SHE WHAT?

YEAH, I CAME HOME AND IT WAS GONE. SHE SOLD IT FOR RENT MONEY, I GUESS.

IT WAS HER COUCH, SO I CAN'T REALLY... SAY ANYTHING...

WELL... MAYBE I'LL... UH... SEE YOU... AT BAND PRACTICE?

SO WHY AREN'T YOU SLEEPING IN RAMONA'S HUGE EMPTY BED, AGAIN?

I LEFT MY KEYS INSIDE. I'M LOCKED OUT.

I THINK I'M GONNA MOVE BACK HOME.

SERIOUSLY?

THINKING ABOUT IT.

DO YOU KNOW ANYTHING ABOUT CATS?

I KNOW THEY SMELL LIKE CAT PEE.

COOL, I'LL MAKE A NOTE OF THAT.

I DUNNO, MAYBE HE'S JUST BETTER IN BED.

I'M SURE HE HAS BETTER *HAIR*...

PLEASE STOP.

SHE LEFT YOU FOR A *REASON*, SCOTT, AND UNTIL YOU FIGURE OUT THAT REASON, YOU'LL NEVER BE A MAN.

I'M TRYING NOT TO DWELL, BUT, Y'KNOW, THANKS.

FISHWICH

LOVE YOU.

STOPPP

159

160

JOSEPH ACTUALLY MADE ME A COPY OF THE SEX BOB-OMB ALBUM.

DUNDAS STREET COACH TERMINAL
AROUND 5 PM

CAN YOU BELIEVE IT'S ONLY SEVENTEEN MINUTES LONG? MONTHS OF WORK.

SHRUG

WE MAKE CONCISE STATEMENTS.

I'LL BE LISTENING TO IT APPROXIMATELY 32 TIMES ON THE BUS RIDE NORTH, SO I HOPE WE DON'T SUCK TOO BAD.

YOU'LL BE BACK, RIGHT?

YEAH... SURE.

APOLOGY
ACCEPTED.

GOLDFISH CRACKERS

CONTINUE?

SCOTT'S NEW APARTMENT

170

174

NEXT:
ONE
MORE
TIME!

CREATING
SCOTT PILGRIM
FOR FUN AND PROFIT

By Bryan Lee O'Malley

SCRIPT

I like to write a full script for my books before I ever start drawing them. It looks kind of like the screenplay for a movie. A lot of cartoonists don't script this way, but I feel that I'm, ironically, not very visual-minded. I like words.

THUMBNAIL

After the script is totally finished (which in this case took a shockingly long time), it's time to break things down into comics. First I roughly determine how much content is going to fit on a page, and then I decide how the information will be laid out on the page. I like to draw these thumbnail sketches at a ridiculously small size, maybe an inch and a half high, otherwise I fear I'll spend too much time rendering them. The simpler they are, the better.

LAYOUT

I transfer the layout to a full-size page. I'm working at 9.5" x 14", which involves ruling and cutting a strip from an 11" x 14" sheet. I use Strathmore bristol and lately I like the vellum finish. I generally ink all of the panel borders before any actual drawing.

PENCILS

I work pretty roughly, with a light blue Col-Erase pencil. I like to place my word balloons as soon as possible - I already know where they'll be, from the thumbnail sketch, and often I can just put a balloon in the corner before I even begin to draw the figures.

The final lettering in the book is done with a computer font, and I space out the word balloons with a combination of letters, scribbles and straight lines. It's not the most scientific method, but I'm used to it by now.

When the pencils are done and I'm satisfied, I immediately ink in the word balloon outlines, using a cheap Pilot pen. I like those pens because they have a sharp point with great flexibility. They don't last very long, though.

Sometimes I will end up re-penciling a whole panel after having inked in the balloon outlines, trying to keep the figures in roughly the same location. Sometimes I have to paste in a new panel, when things get really bad.

INKS

Mostly done with a brush and ink (Rosemary & Co, #3 Kolinsky Sable, with Koh-I-Noor drawing ink). Small details are drawn with the cheap Pilot pens again — things like wood grain, branches and leaves, floor tiles, etc.

I add or change certain things without re-penciling at all, like the angles of facial features, decorations and textures that I left blank, and shadows on the furniture and floors.

POST-PRODUCTION

Scanning, lettering, and screentones. Like everything else, these processes have been cobbled together from years of experience, tips and tricks learned from all over the place, and so they're difficult to explain. I use a variety of screentone effects, most of which I created myself in Photoshop, and which I've struggled to master the use of over the years. I'm definitely still struggling, and it'd be great if I had about twice as much time to really do a good job on toning.

WELL, I'M SORRY THAT SHE KICKED YOU OUT.

WHAT? NO.

28
the GLOW

SHE JUST NEEDS SOME TIME ALONE OR WHATEVER.

IT'S A SMALL APARTMENT.

WELL, TAKE YOUR TIME.

GLINT

WA-PIKK

ZRUNCH

THAT WAS LIKE $18 DOLLARS' WORTH OF EYELINER KNIVES!

WHAT THE HELL IS YOUR DEAL?

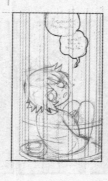

A HANGOVER. REMEMBER? TEQUILA?

AAALL THAT TEQUILA?

KIM PINE (COLD, TIRED AND STILL A LITTLE DRUNK)

ABOUT THE AUTHOR

Bryan Lee O'Malley was made in Canada. This is the first book he has ever completed on schedule. He was 29. It was awesome.

SCOTT 5 PLAYLIST

Beulah - If We Can Land A Man On The Moon, Surely I Can Win Your Heart
Black Lips - Off The Block
Be Your Own Pet - October, First Account
Blondie - Heart Of Glass
The Rolling Stones - Under My Thumb
Neko Case - Lion's Jaws
Lou Reed - Perfect Day (Acoustic Demo)
Art Brut - Fight
Badfinger - Without You
Spoon - I Summon You
Sloan - I'm Not Through With You Yet
Fleetwood Mac - Don't Stop

author illustration by Brandon Graham. comic strip by Corey Lewis.